For my grandsons
Philip, Alexander, and Oliver—K.L.

To Madeleine Edmondson—J.C.

Editor: Wendy Boase
Art Editor: David Bennett

THIS IS A BORZOI BOOK PUBLISHED BY ALFRED A. KNOPF, INC.

Copyright © 1985 by Walker Books Ltd.
Text copyright © 1985 by Alfred A. Knopf, Inc.
Illustrations copyright © 1985 by Kenneth Lilly
All rights reserved under International and Pan-American Copyright
Conventions. Published in the United States by Alfred A. Knopf, Inc., New
York. Distributed by Random House, Inc., New York. Originally published in
two volumes as *Large as Life Daytime Animals* and *Large as Life Nighttime
Animals* by Walker Books Ltd., London, in 1985.
Manufactured in Italy   10   9   8   7   6   5   4   3   2   1
First American Edition

Library of Congress Cataloging-in-Publication Data
Lilly, Kenneth. Large as life animals.
Originally published in two separate volumes as: Large as life daytime animals
life size and Large as life nighttime animals life size. Summary: Brief text
and life-size illustrations present the characteristics of a variety of small diurnal
and nocturnal animals.
ISBN 0-679-80459-5   1. Animals—Pictorial works—Juvenile literature.
2. Nocturnal animals—Pictorial works—Juvenile literature.   [1. Animals.
2. Nocturnal animals] I. Cole, Joanna.   II. Lilly, Kenneth. Large as life
nighttime animals life size.   III. Title.
QL49.L67   1990   591'.022'2   89-15391

Large as Life Animals

IN BEAUTIFUL LIFE-SIZE PAINTINGS

Paintings by Kenneth Lilly

TEXT BY JOANNA COLE

ALFRED A. KNOPF · New York

Little Blue Penguin

The smallest penguins in the world never see ice and snow. Little blue penguins live on the beaches of Australia, not at the South Pole like most other penguins.

These babies would fit easily in your two hands. But they wouldn't want to stay there. They are waddling down to the water for a swimming lesson.

Red Squirrel

This red squirrel is getting ready to jump.
It spreads its legs far apart and leaps from
one tree to another. Its bushy tail comes
in handy for balancing.

   When the squirrel sleeps, it uses its tail
another way. It wraps the tail around
itself like a warm blanket.

Queen Alexandra's Birdwing Butterfly

Live birdwing butterflies are exactly the same size as
this painting of them! The female birdwing is the
largest butterfly you'll ever see.

  The male is smaller than the female. You can see
him standing on a spiky red flower. He is tasting it
at the same time. Butterflies taste with their feet, not
with their tongues!

Lesser Spotted Woodpecker

Why does a woodpecker tap-tap-tap on a tree? It is looking for food. From the sound, the woodpecker can tell if an insect is hidden under the bark. Then it bores a hole and gets the insect out with its long tongue.

Woodpeckers make a larger hole in a tree for their nest.

Common Tree Frog

Most frogs live in ponds. Tree frogs are the only ones that live up high. Sticky pads on their fingers and toes help them climb trees. Their tongues are sticky too, and they use them to catch insects like the ladybug.

 When it rains, the tree frog climbs under a leaf to keep dry.

Eastern Chipmunk

Chipmunks don't wear clothes, but they do have pockets. Inside each cheek is a roomy pouch for nuts and seeds. One small chipmunk can carry seventeen nuts at once!

Black-tailed Prairie Dog

These roly-poly animals aren't dogs.
They are a kind of squirrel. They are
called prairie dogs because they live
on the American prairies and "talk" to
each other with barking sounds.

When this prairie dog family hears a
warning bark, they will all dive into
their burrows until the danger is past.

Bee Hummingbird

Its fast-beating wings make it hum like a bee. It sips nectar from flowers like a bee. But it is not a bee. It is the smallest bird in the world.

The bee hummingbird weighs less than half a teaspoon of sugar. Its nest is the size of a thimble. In fact, the bee hummingbird is so small it has to be careful not to get caught in a spider's web!

Ermine

The ermine doesn't seem to be hiding, but it is. Its white fur blends in with the snow. The ermine makes its living by hunting mice and other small animals. Camouflage – blending in – helps it sneak up on its prey.

   When summer comes, the ermine changes its color and its name. Its coat turns brown and people call it a stoat.

Squirrel Monkey

Is there a yellow monkey almost as small as a banana? Yes, a squirrel monkey. This mother squirrel monkey would fit inside your school bag. And her baby could go in your pocket.

The monkeys' yellowish green color matches the trees where they live in the rain forests of South America.

Brown Hare

It would be hard to cuddle this big bunny. The brown hare is as big as a dog and very strong. It's a fast runner and a high jumper. Some people say they have seen a brown hare jump over a horse!

Greater Indian Fruit Bat

In the darkness of night, this enormous bat
flies from tree to tree, plucking fruit.
It squeezes out the juice and pulp in its
mouth and swallows, then spits out the
seeds as it flies.

  The fruit bat is one of the largest bats in
the world. When its wings are spread out,
they measure five feet from tip to tip.

Chinchilla

Chinchillas are wild relatives of guinea pigs. In the Andes mountains of South America, chinchillas come out of their dens at dusk to scamper about in the cold night air. They are kept warm by their fur, which is the softest and thickest in the world. It is so dense that fleas cannot live in it!

Giant Toad

Can you imagine a live toad as big as
this picture? Giant toads are so large
that they can hunt mice, birds, and even
snakes. If an enemy tries to bite a giant
toad, it will get a nasty surprise.
The toad's warty skin gives off a poison
that stings.

Wood Mouse

On autumn nights, dainty wood mice
look for food to store for the winter in
their burrows. They are good climbers
and can jump like little kangaroos.

Wood mice are so accustomed to the
dark that even bright moonlight sets
them scurrying for a hiding place.

Royal Antelope

Most antelopes are the size of deer,
but this one is no bigger than a rabbit.
One royal antelope at a zoo was so
tiny its legs were as thin as pencils,
and all four of its hoofprints fit on a
fifty-cent piece!

Fennec Fox

The fennec fox is a desert animal.
During the heat of the day, it stays in
cool underground tunnels. At night it
comes out to hunt. It catches some mice
and birds, but lives mainly on insects.

   With its extra-big ears, the tiny fennec
fox can hear insects moving about –
even underground.

Elf Owl

By day, elf owls sleep in holes high in a giant cactus. At night, they fly silently through the air, hunting for food. With its large, round eyes, an owl can see well on the darkest nights. It can also turn its head in an almost complete circle to see directly behind itself.

The elf owl is one of the world's smallest owls. When it first hatches from the egg, an elf owlet could fit on a postage stamp!

Western European Hedgehog

These baby hedgehogs eagerly lap up a
saucer of milk someone has left for them.
They don't often get milk in the wild.
Their usual foods are slugs, insects, and
earthworms.

The spine-covered hedgehog has a trick
to defend itself against enemies.
It simply rolls itself up into a prickly ball,
protecting its head, legs, and soft belly.

Lesser Mouse Lemur

By day, mouse lemurs sleep curled up like a ball. At night they catch insects and eat small fruits. Sometimes they even eat flowers.

In spite of their name, mouse lemurs are not mice. They are really tiny cousins of monkeys.

Nature Notes

Red Squirrel
(Sciurus vulgaris)

The red squirrel is nimble, busy, agile, and completely at home in the trees. It jumps with ease, can cling to the smoothest bark, and always hurtles head-first down tree trunks. Sometimes it hangs by its clawed hind feet, its thick tail giving it balance. A squirrel's tail can measure 8 inches, almost as long as its whole body. Different kinds of red squirrels live in woods, parks, and bushy fields in Europe, North America, and Japan. They come to the ground only to find food and to bury nuts and acorns for the winter. Hazelnuts are favorites. Red squirrels do not hibernate, but in very cold weather they huddle together in nests, wrapping their tails around themselves for warmth.

Little Blue Penguin
(Eudyptula minor)

Steering with its tail and feet and using its wings as paddles, the little blue penguin is as quick and agile in water as a fish. But penguins are birds, although they cannot fly. Unlike most penguins, however, the little blue lives in warm waters and on sandy beaches, sometimes walking over a mile inland to lay its eggs. The world's smallest penguin, it is found on the southern coasts of Australia and New Zealand and islands nearby. For a flightless bird generally less than 16 inches tall, life on the beach is dangerous. Both the penguin and its eggs are at the mercy of cats, dogs, foxes, rats, ferrets, snakes, and gulls. Chicks, if they survive, are eight or nine weeks old before they learn to swim. Then life is much safer!

Queen Alexandra's Birdwing Butterfly
(Ornithoptera alexandrae)

In the rain forests of Papua New Guinea the chenille plant, with its spikes of small red flowers, is one of many plants that provide food for birdwing butterflies. A butterfly sips nectar from flowers with its long coiled tongue, called a proboscis. The biggest and heaviest butterfly in the world is the female Queen Alexandra. She weighs over 3½ ounces and has a wingspan of up to 12 inches. The male is much smaller but makes up for this with brilliant colors. Birdwings fly with slow rhythmic wing-beats and short glides, usually high in the treetops. Few birds or insects bother them because their bold colors and patterns show that they don't taste good. They have more to fear from butterfly collectors.

Common Tree Frog
(Hyla arborea)

Tree frogs like to sit on stems and sun themselves, but if they get too hot or the weather changes, they jump nimbly underneath the leaves. These tiny frogs, only 2 inches in length, are very skillful acrobats. With their long hind legs they can jump and catch insects in midair; their webbed feet help them to make parachute-style landings; the adhesive pads on their fingers and toes allow them to cling to the slenderest branches. The common tree frog lives in marshes, reedy banks, damp meadows, and gardens in most of Europe and some parts of Asia. In spring the females lay about 1,000 tiny eggs at a time, in clumps the size of walnuts. The tadpoles, when they hatch, are less than ¼ inch long!

Lesser Spotted Woodpecker
(Dendrocopus minor)

This woodpecker is just 5½ inches long, but it drums and drills with the energy of birds twice its size. It taps trees in search of grubs, beetles, and caterpillars to eat. It also eats fruit and seeds. The red-capped male drums rapidly to proclaim his territory or to attract a mate. With their long pointed beaks, both male and female drill and gouge out their nest-hole high up in a branch. Like all woodpeckers, the lesser spotted is a good climber, using its stiff tail as a prop. It hardly ever perches or lands on the ground. Shock-absorbent tissue between its beak and skull prevents the bird from getting severe headaches. Its rat-a-tat-tat can be heard in orchards, parks, and open woodland all over Europe, in England, and in parts of Asia and North Africa.

Black-tailed Prairie Dog
(Cynomys ludovicianus)

This animal is a burrowing squirrel and not a dog at all. It is named for its doglike yelp, as well as for the color of its tail. Prairie dogs live in underground colonies on the plains of North America. The basic group is the family, of perhaps ten animals, who eat, sleep, and play together. Each family digs its own set of tunnels, with several entrances or exits. Above ground, sentries watch constantly for danger. The prairie dog, 12 inches long and weighing only 2 pounds, has many enemies: snakes, eagles, hawks, coyotes, ferrets – and farmers, who destroy it because it eats their crops. In winter, when snow covers the ground, prairie dogs curl up and hibernate until spring.

Eastern Chipmunk
(Tamias striatus)

Chipmunks are frisky, inquisitive animals, but very cautious. At the first sign of danger, they scamper for their burrows. The chipmunk is a kind of squirrel that lives underground. This type of chipmunk is found in forests in eastern parts of North America. When they excavate their burrows, chipmunks are careful to hide their activity. They carry the earth away in their cheek pouches and scatter it in the bushes. These cheek pouches can also hold an astonishing amount of food. As winter approaches, chipmunks collect nuts, acorns, and seeds. In the far north they sleep right through winter in a state of hibernation. Chipmunks can be tamed and make lively pets. For an animal about 10 inches from head to tail, even a watering can is a home big enough for two!

Bee Hummingbird
(Mellisuga helenae)

The bee hummingbird's tiny wings beat so rapidly that only a blur and a bee-like hum tell you that it has wings at all!
Bee hummingbirds can fly backward, forward, up, down, or sideways at great speed. They loop and roll and dive as expertly as stunt pilots. They even drink and bathe in flight by skimming over wet leaves. These birds spend most of their day hovering at flowers such as the hibiscus, sucking up the sweet nectar that gives them energy. They have beautiful iridescent feathers that glitter and flash in the sunlight, but the male, with his red head, is more brilliant than the female. Both birds are under 2 inches long. The bee hummingbird lives in woodlands, shrubberies, and gardens in Cuba.

Squirrel Monkey
(Saimiri sciureus)

Squirrel monkeys are inquisitive, active, noisy, quarrelsome, and extremely agile. In the rain forests of South and Central America, they live and travel in groups of up to 100, leaping swiftly through the trees in single file as if playing follow-the-leader. They use their tails for balance when jumping and for support if they stop to rest. The tail is longer than the whole body, which is less than 12 inches in length. Squirrel monkeys spend nearly all their time in trees, catching insects, tree frogs, and snails; stealing birds' eggs; and snatching berries, nuts, and fruit to eat. They are easily tamed and, with their appealing features and acrobatic talents, are popular pets. The biggest pet squirrel monkeys ride easily on the backs of the local dogs!

Ermine
(Mustela erminea)

Ermine is the name given to a stoat when it has shed its brown summer coat and grown a winter one, which is usually pure white except for the black tip of the tail. Perfectly camouflaged against the snow, the ermine hunts rabbits, hares, mice, voles, small birds, fish, and reptiles. Although it is less than 18 inches long including its tail, the ermine is a very fierce hunter. But because it hunts gamebirds and domestic poultry, farmers lay traps for it. It is also killed for its snowy fur. Ermines live in many wild places, as well as near farms, in the British Isles, Europe, North America, and northern Asia. Ermines are alert, energetic, and immensely curious animals, leaping, tumbling, and wrestling in play, and often standing up on their hind legs when hunting.

Greater Indian Fruit Bat
(Pteropus giganteus)

By day thousands of fruit bats roost together in the forests and scrubland of Southeast Asia. At sunset they take to the air, like a huge black cloud. These bats have superb night vision and a keen sense of smell. On their vast wings, up to 5 feet across, they fly off in search of wild figs, mangoes, bananas, and other fruit to eat. Fruit bats are slow but powerful fliers. They use their feet and clawed thumbs to cling to branches. In the early morning the bats return to "camp" to sleep. There is much quarreling, fidgeting, and yawning before they settle down, hanging by one or both feet, with their heads on their breasts and wings wrapped around their bodies. The fruit bat is also called a flying fox because of its foxlike head.

Brown Hare
(Lepus capensis)

Brown hares are native to Europe and Africa, and have been taken to other continents. They live in fields and woods, on moors and sand dunes, often close to cultivated land. Each hare has its own territory, crossed by its private paths which it keeps in order by biting off straggly plants. Sometimes hares are seen during the day, but mostly they rest then and feed at night. They eat all kinds of grasses, flowers, roots, berries, fruit, and vegetables. When danger threatens, hares freeze until the last moment, then shoot off with a mighty leap and a great burst of speed. Brown hares, which measure 18 to 30 inches, are hunted by foxes, wild cats, weasels, birds of prey, and humans.
In March, during the mating season, male hares leap, box, kick, and chase each other with spectacular energy.

Chinchilla
(Chinchilla laniger)

The chinchilla's fur is incredibly soft, and each hair splits into about 20 finer hairs, so fine that they are almost invisible to the naked eye. Chinchillas have been hunted almost to extinction for their beautiful fur. Now they are protected by law, but they are rare in the wild. Chinchillas live in small groups high up in the Andes mountains in Chile and Bolivia. At sunset they come out of their dens and hop rapidly about on tiny feet, tails held in a tight curl. A chinchilla's tail can measure up to 6 inches; its body is between 9 and 11 inches long. Chinchillas nibble on any vegetation they can find, but at the least alarm they give a loud cry and scamper for the safety of their dens.

Wood Mouse
(Apodemus sylvaticus)

The wood mouse is an agile climber and an excellent runner and jumper. It moves incredibly quickly and, when surprised, leaps and bounds with great energy. Its tail is about as long as its whole body, which can be up to 4 inches. This tiny rodent inhabits woodland, scrub, gardens, and hedgerows in Europe, North Africa, and parts of Asia. (The North American deer mouse is very similar.) Wood mice spend the day underground in a complex system of tunnels and chambers. At night they come out to feed on seeds, berries, insects, worms, and spiders. They are also fond of fruit. In autumn wood mice hoard food in their burrows, which helps them to survive the winter.

Giant Toad
(Bufo marinus)

This massive toad, 4 to 10 inches long and weighing well over 2 pounds, has an enormous appetite. It will eat any live food it can swallow – from insects and beetles to mice, birds, and snakes. During the day giant toads shelter in damp places, in holes, or under leaves, logs, and stones. At dusk they come out in search of food. Giant toads live near pools and swamps around houses, gardens, and fields in southern Texas, Mexico, and Central and South America. They have also been taken to most countries where sugarcane is grown, because they prey on sugar beetles. Like many other toads, the giant toad fills itself up with air when frightened. An animal that swallows a giant toad will suffocate when the toad puffs up, if it hasn't already been poisoned.

Fennec Fox
(Fennecus zerda)

The fennec is the smallest fox and has the largest ears. Its body measures about 14 inches and its ears 6 inches or more. Its hearing is so sharp that it can locate insects under the sand by listening for their tiny movements. The fennec lives in North Africa and the Middle East and is also called the desert fox. It feeds mainly on insects, especially locusts, but will also eat rats, lizards, birds and their eggs, plant roots, and fruit. Any food not eaten is buried; in the desert nothing is wasted. When the fox leaves its burrow, it uses its bushy tail to protect its head from the heat. Its large ears radiate heat to help keep it cool. At night, when the temperature drops, its thick, silky fur keeps it warm.

Royal Antelope
(Neotragus pygmaeus)

The smallest antelope in the world is no bigger than a hare. In West Africa, where it lives, it is called the king of the hares, and is thought to be especially nimble and clever. It knows its territory well, and its small size enables it to scurry away unseen from animals, birds, snakes, or humans who prey on it. The royal antelope's remarkable jumping ability also makes it difficult to catch. When startled, it can cover 10 feet in a single bound, yet it is only 10 inches tall! These shy, secretive animals are active in the forest at dusk or by night, when they feed on leaves, buds, shoots, fungi, fruit, and grass. Occasionally royal antelopes make daring nighttime raids on vegetable gardens and cocoa or peanut plantations.

Elf Owl
(Microthene whitneyi)

This little owl is seen in woodland, but is most common in desert areas, where its favorite nesting site is a woodpecker's hole high up in the giant saguaro cactus. The elf owl is only 6 inches long. The saguaro, which is found in the southwestern USA and Mexico, is the world's biggest cactus, and can grow to 50 feet. During the day the elf owl sits motionless in its hole or in dense foliage. At dusk it flies out to feed, just as the woodpeckers come home to sleep. The elf owl's night flight is swift and silent. Its hearing and eyesight are exceptionally keen. The tiny bird usually moves quickly from branch to branch, perching and then pouncing on insects, small reptiles, and rodents.

Western European Hedgehog
(Erinaceus europaeus)

This hedgehog, which is found in western Europe, has a jaunty walk and a confident manner. It knows that by rolling into a ball and erecting its spines, it can frustrate most enemies. The hedgehog has about 16,000 spines on its back! The little hedgehog – between 5 and 11 inches long – is noisy. It snuffles and snorts while hunting for food and sometimes snores loudly in its nest. The hedgehog builds a nest of moss and leaves under bushes and tree roots, often in city parks and gardens. It sleeps there during the day and at night patrols its territory, searching for slugs, snails, beetles, and worms, although it will eat almost anything it comes across. In winter hedgehogs hibernate. When the temperature drops, the hedgehog rolls itself up and goes to sleep for about six months.

Lesser Mouse Lemur
(Microcebus murinus)

Mouse lemurs are noisy, nimble, acrobatic animals that live in the dense forests of Madagascar. Strong fingers and toes give them a firm grip in the topmost branches, and stout tails help them to keep their balance. A lesser mouse lemur's tail is as long as its whole body – 5 to 6 inches. Large ears and eyes enable it to locate insects to feed on in the dark. Mouse lemurs also eat fruit, leaves, and flowers. During the day they sleep, as many as 15 animals in one leafy nest or tree hole. In the hot, dry season mouse lemurs sleep most of the time, living off the fat stored in their bodies and tails.